ACHINES

WITHDRAWN

TRAINS

by Wendy Strobel Dieker

AMICUS | AMICUS INK

track

engine

Look for these
words and pictures
as you read.

passenger
car

tank car

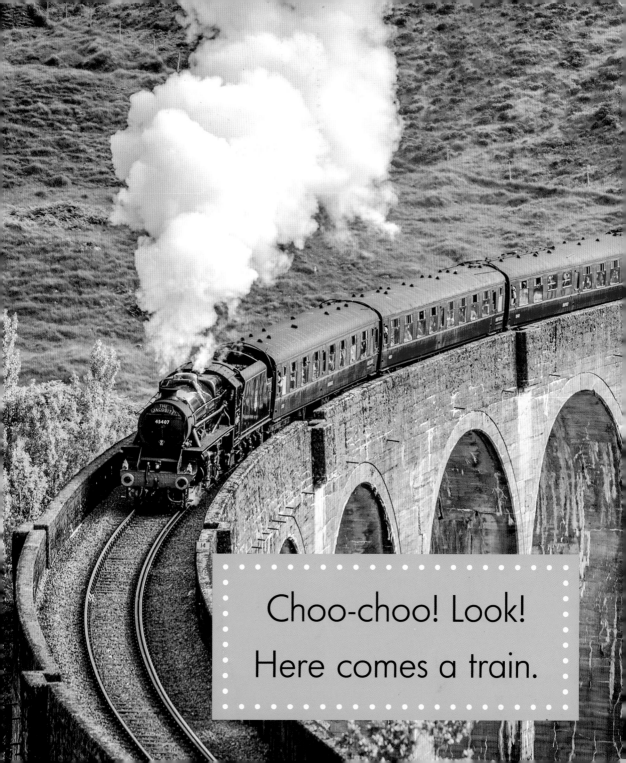

Choo-choo! Look!

Here comes a train.

The train rolls into the station.
It is ready for people to board.

track

See the track?
It is made of steel.
The train's wheels ride on it.

See the engine?

It pulls the cars.

Long trains need two engines.

engine

See the tank car?

It carries oil.

tank car

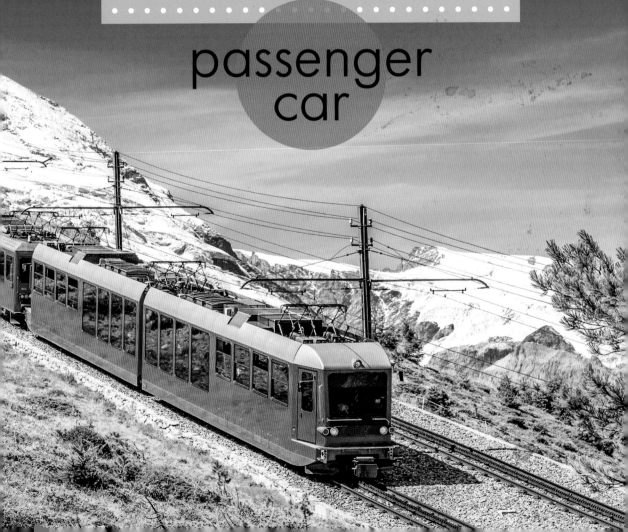

See the passenger car?
People ride in it.

passenger
car

All aboard!
The train is leaving the station.

See the track?
It is made of steel.
The train's wheels ride on it.

track

See the engine?
It pulls the cars.
Long trains need two engines.

engine

track

engine

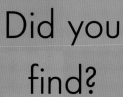

Did you find?

passenger car

tank car

See the passenger car?
People ride in it.

passenger car

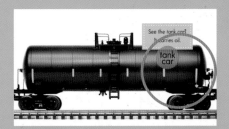

See the tank car?
It carries oil.

tank car

Spot is published by Amicus and Amicus Ink
P.O. Box 1329, Mankato, MN 56002
www.amicuspublishing.us

Library of Congress Cataloging-in-Publication Data
Names: Dieker, Wendy Strobel, author.
Title: Trains / by Wendy Strobel Dieker.
Description: Mankato, Minnesota : Amicus, [2020] | Series:
 Spot. Mighty machines | Audience: K to grade 3.
Identifiers: LCCN 2018024612 (print) | LCCN
 2018036469 (ebook) | ISBN 9781681517315 (pdf)
 | ISBN 9781681516493(library binding) | ISBN
 9781681524351(pbk.) Subjects: LCSH: Railroad trains
 --Juvenile literature. | Railroad trains--Parts--Juvenile
 literature. | Railroads--Juvenile literature. | CYAC: Railroad
 trains. | Railroads. | LCGFT: Instructional and educational
 works. | Picture books. Classification: LCC TF148 (ebook)
 | LCC TF148 .D54 2020 (print) | DDC 625.1--dc23
 LC record available at https://lccn.loc.gov/2018024612

Printed in China

HC 10 9 8 7 6 5 4 3 2 1
PB 10 9 8 7 6 5 4 3 2 1

Alissa Thielges, editor
Deb Miner, series designer
Aubrey Harper, book designer
Holly Young, photo researcher

Photos by Alamy/devi cover, 16; Alamy/
Panupong Ponchai 1; iStock/miroslav_1
3; Shutterstock/Denis Belitsky 4–5;
Getty/aerogondo 6–7; Shutterstock/
Hit1912 8–9; Shutterstock/John Brueske
10–11; Shutterstock/emperorcosar
12–13; iStock/CHBD 14–15

TRAINS

9